Highlands

Sally Morgan & Pauline Lalor

SIMON & SCHUSTER
YOUNG BOOKS

Our planet has many different environments in which a rich variety of plants and animals make their homes. These environments are unique, but they are all under threat — from the growing human population, its industry and its pollution. Young readers can't protect fragile environments unless they understand them. The Living World gives insight into these special areas and makes positive suggestions for their future management.

Commissioning editor: Daphne Butler
Book editor: Claire Llewellyn
Design and artwork: SPL Design
Photographs: Ecoscene, except
Survival Anglia (21t, 22b)
Zefa (9t, 20, 22t, 23)
Typesetting and layout: Quark Xpress

First published in Great Britain in 1992
by Simon & Schuster Young Books

Simon & Schuster Young Books
Campus 400, Maylands Avenue
Hemel Hempstead, Herts HP2 7EZ

© 1992 Simon & Schuster Young Books

All rights reserved

Printed and bound in Belgium
by Proost International Book Production

A catalogue record for this book
is available from the British Library
ISBN 0 7500 1097 5

(Opposite title page)
The mouflon is a wild sheep which lives high on the mountains. It is able to leap from rock to rock.

Contents

Rising high	6-7
Making mountains	8-9
Glaciers and erosion	10-11
Changeable weather	12-13
Changing plant life	14-15
Meadows and moors	16-17
At the top	18-19
Highland animals	20-21
Surviving the cold	22-23
Living in high places	24-25
Highlands under threat	26-27
Planning for the future	28-29
Index	30

6 Rising high

What are highlands?

Highlands are huge areas of land where there are mountains. When the ground rises higher than the rest of the land it is called a hill. If it rises more than 1000 metres and has steep slopes then it is called a mountain. Most mountains were formed hundreds of millions of years ago, but some are still being made today.

There are mountain ranges in every continent in the world. Some of them are labelled on the map. ▼

Where do we find highlands?

Highlands are found all over the world, usually in groups called mountain ranges. They form some of the most spectacular scenery on Earth. Many of the tallest peaks are covered in snow all year round. The biggest range is the Himalayas which stretches for thousands of kilometres across six countries in central Asia.

The Himalayas near to Mount Everest which is the highest mountain in the world at 8,848 metres. ▶

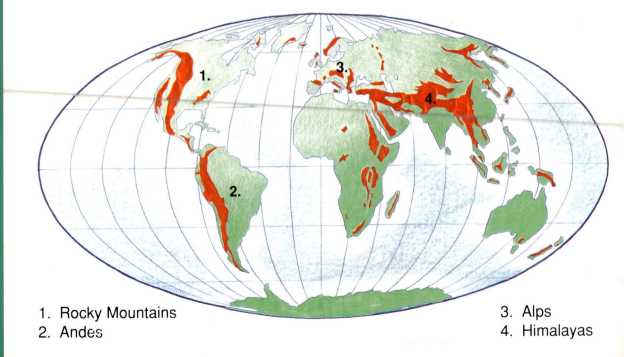

1. Rocky Mountains
2. Andes
3. Alps
4. Himalayas

7

8  Making mountains

▲ *Mountain ranges like the Alps form slowly over millions of years.*

Solid ground?

We like to think that the Earth is solid and unchanging, but it isn't. The centre of the planet is made of very hot dense rock. The thin outer skin is much cooler and forms a crust. The ground we live on is on top of the crust. Although the ground seems solid and still, it isn't always.

The Earth's crust

The Earth's crust is like a huge cracked eggshell. We call the pieces of this shell 'plates'. The plates move very slowly on the hot rock below. Occasionally, we are reminded that the ground moves by news of an earthquake.

How mountains are made

It takes millions of years for mountains to form, because mountain building is linked to the way the plates move slowly over the surface of the Earth. In some places the plates push against each other making the rocks buckle up, forming mountain ranges thousands of kilometres long. This is how mountain ranges like the Himalayas, Rockies and Alps were formed.

▲ An erupting volcano spurts out hot, molten rock which hardens as it cools.

Volcanoes

The stresses in the rocks under the ground are very great. Sometimes, hot, molten rock forces its way up, and spills out over the surface where it cools and becomes rock again. We call the liquid rock lava. As more and more lava erupts and hardens, a cone-shaped mountain grows higher and higher. We call this mountain a volcano.

▲ The typical cone shape of a volcanic mountain. This one is in Chile, South America.

10 Glaciers and erosion

The shape of mountains is always changing, little by little. The rock is slowly worn down by wind, rain, rivers and frost, and by the most powerful force of all—moving ice. This wearing down is called erosion.

Why so much ice?

As winds blow across the seas and oceans, water is picked up from the surface and carried away by the wind. Clouds form and when the wind reaches land, rain falls. High up on a mountain the air is much colder than it is at the foot, so the rain falls as snow.

New falls of snow cover older snow and crush the bottom layers into a solid mass of ice, much the same as when you make snowballs. In some places, more and more ice collects in a sheet. It becomes so big and heavy that it starts to move slowly downhill, just like a river but much more slowly. This is a glacier.

◀ *A glacier moves slowly downhill like a river of ice.*

Rivers of ice

Glaciers form high in the mountains. As they slowly move downhill, their great weight grinds away at the rock below. Over hundreds of years they cut into the sides of the mountain making deep, wide valleys. Lower down the mountain the tip of the glacier melts and water runs away to form an icy cold river.

Tumbling down the mountainside, this stream has formed from the melting tip of a glacier. The water is icy cold. ▼

12 Changeable weather

Warm days and cold nights

There are enormous differences in the highlands between day and night-time temperatures. During the day it may be hot, and at night almost freezing. The higher you go up the mountain the bigger the differences in temperature.

◄ *Villages are usually found on the slopes that face the sun, which are much warmer.*

Sudden changes in the weather like this can be dangerous. How would you dress if you were climbing a mountain? ▼

Winter snow and summer sun

When you think of mountains you probably imagine deep snow, biting winds and bitter cold. Winter can be very severe, but between the storms it is usually clear and bright and the sun feels hot even though the ground is frozen.

The warmer spring weather melts the snow on the lower slopes. The weather in summer may be much hotter, but it can still be changeable—one minute clear and sunny, and the next raining with the mountain wrapped in dense cloud.

14  Changing plant life

Trees in the valleys

As you climb up a mountain you notice that the plants begin to change. Those that grow at the foot of the mountain cannot grow at the top. The valleys and the lower slopes are often covered by forests. Trees can suffer in bad weather because they grow high above the ground. In highlands the tops of the taller trees are exposed to the wind and cold, and the heavy weight of the snow breaks their branches.

Deciduous trees grow on the lowest slopes. They lose their leaves in winter, so the cold and snow do not damage them.

Coniferous forests

Most of the trees in the highlands are conifers. They can grow higher up the mountain than deciduous trees because they are better adapted to the cold. They are evergreen, and have tough leaves that are shaped like needles. Their branches slope downward so the snow slips off easily.

Conifers have tough needle-shaped leaves which can survive the winter weather. ▸

◂ *The leaves on deciduous trees change colour before they fall. The forests are a spectacular sight in autumn.*

Trees are only able to grow on the lower slopes. Above the tree line trees are replaced by smaller plants. ▸

Tree line

As you climb higher, you leave the trees behind. There is a line on every mountain above which trees cannot grow because the cold and wind are too severe. This is called the tree line, and here you will see the greatest change in vegetation.

16 Meadows and moors

Flower meadows

High up on the cold steep slopes of a mountain the soil is thin. Here you would not expect to see flowers, but where there are meadows above the tree line, a wide variety of grasses and plants grow. In early summer, their flowers make patches of vivid colour.

In early summer the meadows are full of scent and colour. Insects pollinate the flowers as they feed on the nectar. ▼

Sweet scents

Summer is quite short in highlands and there are only a few months when the upper slopes are free of snow. The plants found here must grow fast and produce their flowers very quickly. The sweet nectar inside the flowers attracts thousands of insects which transfer pollen from one flower to another as they feed.

Heather moor and peat bog

Sometimes, the rock and soil of the highlands are too poor for meadows, and are covered by moorland. Trees cannot grow here, but there are lots of small shrubs. Much of the Scottish Highlands are like this. Heather grows everywhere, and in late summer the moors are coloured by its pink and purple flowers. Rainwater may drain away very slowly on this kind of land, and wet areas called peat bogs form. Mosses and rushes grow here, and small trees like the dwarf birch.

▲ *Peat bogs and ponds have formed where the water cannot drain away.*

Heather is an evergreen plant and an important food for birds like grouse. ▼

18 At the top

Very few plants can survive among the rocks at the top of a mountain. It is too cold and windy, and snow covers the ground for much of the year.

Lichens and mosses

On the very highest, most exposed slopes near the peak, only lichens can survive. They form a brightly coloured crust over the surface of the rock. When they die, they make a thin soil in which plants like mosses can begin to grow.

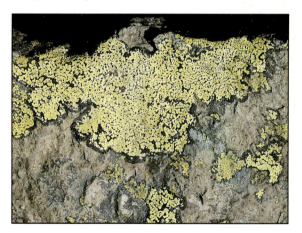

▲ This brightly-coloured crust is a lichen growing slowly across the rock.

◄ Only low-growing plants survive among the highest rocks.

Battle against the cold

Low down among the rocks you can find small, cushion-like plants which hug the ground to avoid the full force of the wind. Their long roots help them to get a good grip on the thin soil and to take up water from such dry ground. The plants can survive through the winter beneath the snow, but they grow very slowly and as a result only produce one or two new leaves each year.

Dwarf willow grows between rocks. It will survive the winter beneath a thick layer of snow. ▼

20  Highland animals

Many nimble animals live high up in the mountains, leaping from rock to rock as they search for food.

Looking for plants

Animals that eat only plants are called herbivores. There are plenty of plants for herbivores in the valleys, but only a few animals can find enough food higher up.

▲ High but safe—few predators are as nimble as the mountain goats which live on the higher slopes.

Large, heavy animals like yaks look for tough low-growing plants on the gentler slopes of the Himalayas. Mountain goats are more skilful climbers. They feed on lichens and grasses high up on craggy cliff faces.

Escaping from predators

The higher goats climb, the safer they are. There are very few large predators in highland areas—only large cats like the mountain lion which hunts mountain goats, and the snow leopard which hunts ibex, another kind of goat which lives in the Himalayas.

Gliding birds

The strong gusting winds make flying difficult for many birds. Eagles and vultures are best adapted to highland living as they have long wings which are suitable for gliding. The wind carries them up to the highest peaks where they glide above the slopes. Their sharp eyes can spot their prey far below—small mammals like marmots and hares—and they drop on them like a stone.

Marmots feed on plants in the meadows. They can stand on their back legs to watch for eagles above.

▲ *Eagles glide over the highlands looking for prey, which they grasp in their strong claws.*

22  Surviving the cold

Mountain animals have to be very hardy if they are to find food and survive the harsh winter weather.

Woolly coats

Animals that live on mountains have very thick, woolly coats which stop their body heat from escaping. The mountain goat can live at great heights because its coat will keep it warm even if the temperature sinks to −40°C. Understandably the wool from these goats is highly prized and makes very warm clothing.

▲ The thick coat of these mountain goats keeps in their body heat.

◀ *The black bear finds a safe place in which to hibernate.*

▲ *Llamas live in the Andes. Their woolly coat helps them survive the bitter cold.*

A long winter sleep

In winter it's so cold, and there is so little food, that many mammals go to sleep until spring. This is called hibernation.

During the autumn mammals such as marmots and bears eat a lot of food which is stored in their bodies as fat. They then find a safe place, like a hole in the ground or a cave, and go into a very deep sleep. Their heart beats much more slowly than usual and the temperature of their body is much cooler. As they sleep they lose a lot of weight because they are living on the fat which is stored in their bodies.

In spring, when the weather gets warmer they wake up and emerge from their hiding place, desperately hungry.

24 Living in high places

The effects of the air

As you climb higher and higher up a mountain, the air becomes thinner. Thin air contains less oxygen, and it can soon make you feel breathless, dizzy and sick. However, people who live in highlands, like the Sherpas of the Himalayas, do not have this problem. Over thousands of years they have developed larger hearts and lungs. With each breath they are able to inhale more air, which provides them with the oxygen their bodies need.

Farming the slopes

The higher slopes of mountains are the harshest places to live, so very few people make their homes there. Most people live lower down in the sheltered valleys, and farm what land they can.

The main crops are hay, barley and potatoes. On warm, sheltered slopes there may be orchards and vineyards. Many farmers keep cattle, too. The meadows above the tree line are used for grazing in the summer, but in winter the cattle are brought back down to the valleys and kept in barns.

In South America, the Quechua Indians farm llamas. These useful animals carry goods across the Andes Mountains, and their warm wool is made into clothing.

Farmers make the best use they can of the sloping land above their village. ▶

◀ *Hard work like this would be exhausting for people from the lowlands. They would feel breathless and dizzy in the thin mountain air.*

Highlands under threat

Few people live in highland areas and there has been little damage to this environment—until recently. Now, highlands are under threat from acid rain, deforestation and tourism.

Deforestation

Huge areas of mountain forest are being cut down. This is called deforestation and it is being carried out to clear land for farming or building.

Trees protect the environment in a very important way. The roots which anchor the tree in the ground also hold the soil together and prevent it from being washed away by heavy rains.

If the forests are cut down, the soil covering the whole slope may be washed away forever. Nothing can then grow on the eroded slopes. Not only that, in very wet weather the soil holds a lot of water; without the soil the water will simply run off the hillsides and flood the valleys.

Acid rain

Industries in countries far away from highlands produce harmful gases from their factory chimneys. Winds blow these gases to highlands where they mix with water droplets in clouds. These then fall as rain—acid rain as it is called—which damages the trees until they eventually die. Huge areas of highland forests have been destroyed in this way.

Tourism and sport

Highlands are being spoilt by tourism and sport, especially skiing. New ski runs and lifts carve out huge tracks and destroy the grassy slopes. Meadows are disappearing under the new hotels and roads which are being built for the tourists. New resorts in unspoilt valleys destroy the habitats of thousands of plants and animals. How can they be protected?

More and more people are taking skiing holidays. As new ski lifts and hotels are built, meadows and forests are destroyed.

27

28 Planning the future

There are several ways in which the highlands can be protected

Planting

More damage has been caused by cutting down trees than by any other action. A good way to prevent further damage is to replant the trees. This would stop soil erosion. Some countries, like Nepal, cannot afford to replant their forests and must be helped by the richer countries of the world.

Terracing

As water moves downhill it picks up speed and carries more soil. One way to stop the water moving downhill so quickly is to build steps or terraces into the hillside. This reduces soil erosion. Today, more and more farmers are terracing their slopes.

The slopes behind this Himalayan village have been deforested. Terracing the hillside will at least slow down the soil erosion.

The animals and plants which live in this National Park in the Rocky Mountains are protected by law.

National Parks

Highlands are places of great beauty. They can be protected by making them National Parks— areas where building and tourism is strictly controlled and where animals and plants are protected. In North America large areas of the Rocky Mountains are now National Parks. Here tourists can enjoy the mountains, but without damaging them.

Index

acid rain 26
animals 20, 21, 22, 24, 26
autumn 14, 15

birds 17, 21

deforestation 26, 28

Earth's crust 8
Earth's plates 14, 16
erosion 10, 11, 26, 28

farming 24, 25, 26, 28
flowers 16, 17

glaciers 10, 11

hibernation 23
Himalayas 6, 20, 21, 24

meadows 16, 21, 24, 26
moorland 16
mountain ranges 6, 8, 9

National Park 28

plants 14, 16, 17, 19, 20, 26
predators 20, 21

rock 8, 9, 11, 15, 16, 19, 20

soil 16, 19, 26, 28
spring 13, 23
summer 13, 17, 24

tourism 26, 28
tree line 15, 16, 25
trees 14, 15, 16, 26, 28

valleys 11, 14, 20, 24, 26
volcanoes 9

wind 11, 13, 14, 15, 19, 21, 26
winter 13, 14, 19, 22, 23, 24

Mountain scenery: the most spectacular in the world. ▶